OUR GREAT STATES

WHAT'S GREAT ABOUT
SOUTH CAROLINA?

✳ Rebecca Felix

LERNER PUBLICATIONS ✳ MINNEAPOLIS

CONTENTS

Content Consultant: Rod Andrew, Professor of History, Clemson University

Lerner Publications Company
A division of Lerner Publishing Group, Inc.
241 First Avenue North
Minneapolis, MN 55401 USA

For reading levels and more information, look up this title at www.lernerbooks.com.

Main body text set in ITC Franklin Gothic Std Book Condensed 12/15.
Typeface provided by Adobe Systems.

Library of Congress Cataloging-in-Publication Data

Felix, Rebecca, 1984–
        What's great about South Carolina? / by Rebecca Felix.
            pages   cm. — (Our great states)
        Includes index.
            ISBN 978-1-4677-3861-3 (lib. bdg. : alk. paper)
            ISBN 978-1-4677-6263-2 (eBook)
        1. South Carolina—Juvenile literature. I. Title.
F269.3.F45 2015
975.7—dc23   2014019886

Manufactured in the United States of America
1 – PC – 12/31/14

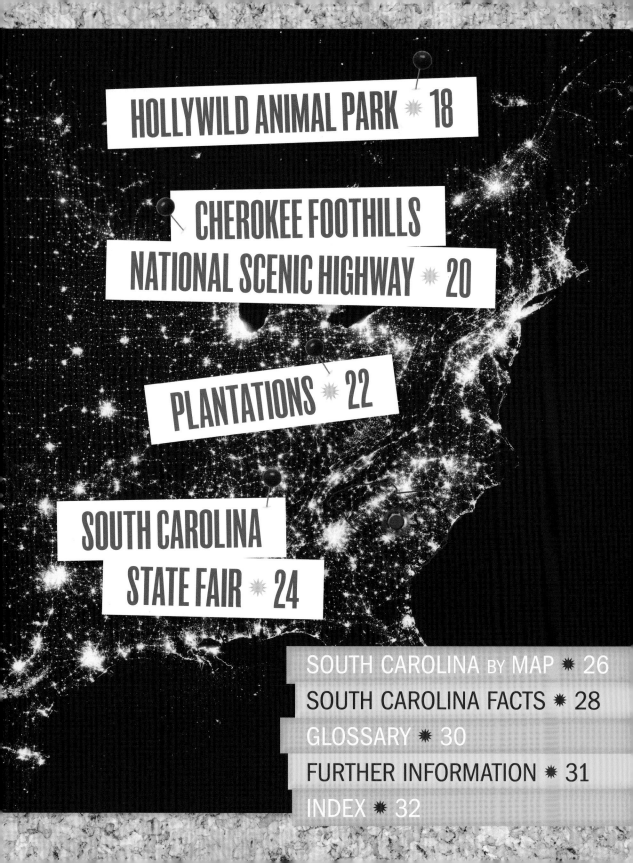

SOUTH CAROLINA Welcomes You!

Does splashing down seaside waterslides sound fun? How about horseback riding? Or hiking through waterfalls? If so, South Carolina is the state for you! Here, historic mansions meet sandy beaches. Forests cover the Blue Ridge Mountains. The state has rolling hills, roller coasters, waterfalls, and water parks. Smell the boiled peanuts and shrimp. Bluegrass music and the Gullah culture are also part of South Carolina's identity. Read on to learn about ten things that make this state great!

APPALACHIAN MOUNTAINS

NORTH CAROLINA

Sassafras Mountain
(3,560 feet/
1,085 m)

Rock Hill

Greenville

PIEDMONT PLATEAU

Great Pee Dee River

N

Columbia

Congaree National Park

Sumter

Myrtle Beach

GEORGIA

Savannah River

(North Fork)

(South Fork)

Santee River

Edisto River

Goose Creek

Mount Pleasant

Summerville

North Charleston

Charleston

ATLANTIC OCEAN

Explore South Carolina's forests and all the places in between. Just turn the page to find out all about the Palmetto State. >

Hilton Head Island

Miles
0   20   40   60
0   40   80
Kilometers

MYRTLE BEACH

> Can you picture 60 miles (97 kilometers) of sandy beaches? You have just pictured the Grand Strand in South Carolina. *Strand* comes from the German word for "beach." The Grand Strand is the most popular strip of sandy beaches along the East Coast. Myrtle Beach is at the center of Grand Strand. This city is bursting with activity! Visit Splashes. It is just one of the city's many amusement parks. It is also a water park. Speed and swoosh down giant slides right by the sea! Myrtle Beach has many mini-golf courses. But Hawaiian Rumble Mini Golf is the only one with smoke and fire! Its course has a fake volcano. It erupts several times an hour.

The main attraction at Myrtle Beach is the beach, of course! Swim and build sandcastles. Or walk the beach's busy boardwalk. It has ice cream shops, stores, and live music. A Kids Carnival is held every Monday night. See fireworks each Wednesday night. The boardwalk is also home to SkyWheel, a huge Ferris wheel. Hop on and view South Carolina sights from up in the sky!

Myrtle Beach's SkyWheel Ferris wheel is 187 feet (57 meters) tall!

Spend the afternoon building sandcastles at Myrtle Beach.

CHARLESTON

> Charleston is a city of historic beauty and modern fun. Do you hear the clip-clop of hooves? It is the sound of horse-drawn carriages. Take a ride on one through the city's Historic District. See curtains of droopy Spanish moss hanging from the trees in Charleston. Would you rather go for a walk? Follow a pirate around town with Charleston Pirate Tours. A costumed pirate and his live parrot are the guides. Listen to real stories of pirate attacks as you tour the city.

After touring the city, visit the South Carolina Aquarium. It has more than seven thousand sea creatures! View them through the huge aquarium window. It is the tallest window in North America. Make sure to check out the 4-D theater before you leave. A movie plays as water splashes and wind swirls around you!

You'll see historic buildings, including mansions, on your horse-drawn carriage ride through Charleston.

The South Carolina Aquarium's sea creatures swim in 385,000 gallons (1.5 million liters) of water!

FORT SUMTER

> A small island off South Carolina's coast holds a lot of history. Fort Sumter is where the first battle of the Civil War (1861–1865) took place. A water taxi takes you to the site. Watch the city of Charleston shrink behind you. Look for dolphins racing in the waves beside the boat!

As the boat lands, look closely at the fort's crumbling brick walls. More than four thousand cannonballs whizzed toward these walls during the site's famous battle. Stop by the island museum. See pictures and learn more about the Battle of Fort Sumter. Back on land, go to the education center in Charleston Harbor. Real newspapers and soldier uniforms from the war are on display.

Stand next to real battle cannons at Fort Sumter.

CIVIL WAR IN SOUTH CAROLINA

Abraham Lincoln was voted president of the United States in 1860. At that time, slavery was common across the South. Many southerners worried slavery would end under Lincoln's leadership. In December, South Carolina seceded from the United States. In the coming weeks and months, so did other southern states. A war began between the Union (North) and the Confederacy (South). The first shots were fired at Fort Sumter. The Union won the US Civil War in 1865.

HILTON HEAD

> Have you ever spied on alligators from atop a horse? You can at Lawton Stables! Lawton Stables is on Hilton Head Island. Visitors eight years old and older can ride horses through the Sea Pines Forest Preserve. Wild gators and island birds can be viewed from the trails. Riders younger than eight years old can ride ponies through an animal farm. It has donkeys, potbellied pigs, rabbits, and more.

Dress up like a pirate for Shannon Tanner's Most Excellent Pirate Expedition. Follow Captain Shannon through Shelter Cove Harbour. Be sneaky! Your destination is the docks. There, you'll help capture a ship. Then you and your rowdy band of pirates will climb aboard. You're headed to a showdown at sea! Fire water cannons to win a treasure map. Will you find the treasure back on land?

Watch for alligators lurking in the Sea Pines Forest Preserve.

Ride your Lawton Stables horse through the Sea Pines Forest Preserve on Hilton Head Island.

GULLAH CELEBRATIONS

> People throughout South Carolina are proud of their Gullah heritage. In Beaufort, the Gullah Festival takes place during one weekend each May. Try the Frogmore stew. It is a traditional Gullah dish. It combines boiled shrimp, sausage, corn, and crab. What would French, English, and African languages sound like blended together? Find out as storytellers share tales in the Gullah language. See dancers in traditional clothing. They move to the sound of African drums. Find games in the Children's Village at this festival.

Beaufort also hosts the Penn Center Heritage Days Celebration. The celebration honors Gullah culture each November. Check out Gullah artwork at the craft fair. Here you'll learn to make traditional Gullah crafts. And don't miss the fish fry and parade!

GULLAH CULTURE

Tiny islands called the Sea Islands dot the Atlantic Coast of South Carolina. They are home to the Gullah culture. The Gullah people are descendants of Sea Island slaves. These slaves made up most of the population on the islands during the 1700s and the 1800s. The Gullah people worked on rice plantations on the Sea Islands. They created their own culture and language. Many Gullah people still live on the islands. Many still speak the Gullah language.

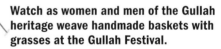

Watch as women and men of the Gullah heritage weave handmade baskets with grasses at the Gullah Festival.

CONGAREE NATIONAL PARK

> Congaree National Park is outside Columbia. The Congaree River floods the area about ten times a year. Look closely for creatures in the park. You might see snakes slithering on the forest floor. Deer and wild hogs are also sometimes seen in the forest. A summer warning: the mosquitoes are thick! It's best to visit in spring or fall.

Canoeing is a great way to check out the park. Reserve a guided canoe tour with a ranger. Rangers also offer Nature Discovery Hikes. There is a program called Skin and Bones. Check out real skulls and furs of Congaree critters! The Owl Prowl is a fun—and slightly spooky—tour. It is a night hike through the forest. Listen for owl calls. Then check out cypress trees that have fungi that glow in the dark!

Watch for river otters as you hike through the floodplains of Congaree National Park.

SOUTH CAROLINA WATER SYSTEMS

South Carolina has eight river basins. Water flows under or on top of these land areas to reach a river. Many types of water ecosystems are formed. Swamps and marshes are two examples. They are areas of land that do not have good water drainage, so standing water collects. These ecosystems form near oceans. They can also form near rivers. Trees grow in swamps. Grasses mainly grow in marshes. Floodplains are on higher land. They are covered in water when a nearby river floods. The rest of the time the ground is often soggy.

Tank, an African white rhino, is the only rhino at Hollywild Animal Park.

HOLLYWILD ANIMAL PARK

> Did you know you could meet TV and movie stars in South Carolina? All types of wild celebrities live in Wellford at the Hollywild Animal Park. They are hired to star in TV commercials, shows, and movies. Meet Tank, an African white rhino. He has been in many TV commercials. Chewy the lion was part of the Walt Disney film *The Lion King*. Artists based the character of Scar in *The Lion King* on him. Several of the chimps have been on TV. And the zebras have starred in a music video!

Hollywild is open between April and December. When you visit, take the Outback Safari Ride. It takes you through acres of land where animals roam. Animal food is available to buy. When the bus stops, animals will eat it right out of your hand! You can even meet one special animal up close. Who knows? You might meet the next Hollywood star!

Bottle-feed calves at Hollywild Animal Park.

CHEROKEE FOOTHILLS NATIONAL SCENIC HIGHWAY

> Highway 11 runs through northwest South Carolina. It is also called Cherokee Foothills National Scenic Byway. Cherokee American Indians used this route centuries ago. So did English and French fur traders. The route winds past the Blue Ridge Mountains. Along the way, you'll find waterfalls and swimming holes.

Hike to Table Rock State Park's Carrick Creek Falls. Stand on a rocky ledge behind the waterfall. Look out through the rushing water. Hop in the waterfall's shallow pool to splash and wade. For deeper swimming, go to the park's Pinnacle Lake. It has a sandy beach and two diving boards. Cannonball!

The next stop is Long Shoals Wayside Park. Here, creek water rushes over a flat, sloping rock. It creates a natural rock waterslide! Visitors slip down the rock slide on floaties, tubes, or their bottoms! The slide spills into a swimming hole.

SOUTH CAROLINA LANDFORMS

South Carolina has six geographic regions. The Blue Ridge Mountains are in the northwest part of the state. The foothills of the mountains have many waterfalls. Next is the Piedmont. It is a large plateau. Sandhills make up the third region. Next are the inner coastal plains and the outer coastal plains. The coastal zone is the sixth region. It borders the ocean.

Carrick Creek Falls offers a shallow pool to swim in at Table Rock State Park.

PLANTATIONS

> South Carolina once had many working plantations. You can tour several of them, including Boone Hall Plantation & Gardens. Let butterflies land on you at the Butterfly Pavilion, where dozens of butterflies fly freely. Life-sized figures are set up in slave cabins. They pair with audio recordings. Listen as they tell what daily life was like for plantation slaves.

Middleton Place is another plantation. It is outside downtown Charleston. Plantation Days are held here each November. Visitors learn many crafts. You can even learn how to turn cotton from the fields into fabric. Magnolia Plantation & Gardens is just minutes from Middleton Place. Ride the plantation Nature Train. It goes past wetlands and slave cabins. Keep your eyes peeled! There are alligators and great blue herons lurking. Get closer to plantation creatures at the Zoo & Nature Center. Feeling brave? Tour the reptile house. Come face-to-face with lizards, turtles, and snakes.

Learn how to make buckets at Middleton Place.

SLAVERY ON SOUTH CAROLINA PLANTATIONS

The Atlantic slave trade occurred between the 1600s and the 1800s. Africans were captured from West Africa and shipped to North America. They were forced into slavery. Slaves worked on rice and cotton plantations in South Carolina. The state's economy soon became based on rice and cotton. More slaves were brought in to work on plantations. Their forced labor built South Carolina's economy.

SOUTH CAROLINA STATE FAIR

> No South Carolina trip is complete without trying special state foods. Riding carnival rides and seeing sandcastles are also musts. You're in luck! All this fun and more is packed into twelve days each October. It's the South Carolina State Fair in Columbia! First up at the fair? Pet or ride camels, ponies, and elephants at the petting zoo. Then watch pigs race to win an Oreo cookie. The fair also has races featuring donkeys and mules.

Try some carnival rides and check out the sand sculpture contest. World champion sculptors compete against one another. They create giant works of art out of tons of sand. Each year has a new theme. Did all that fun make you hungry? Gobble down a piece of fried peach pie. Or try pecan rolls or fried sweet potatoes. And don't forget the boiled peanuts!

YOUR TOP TEN

You just read about ten great things to see and do in South Carolina. If you were planning a trip to South Carolina, what would be on your top ten list? What kind of animals or sights would you like to see? What South Carolina activities sound most exciting? Write down your top ten choices. You can turn your choices into a book just like this one. Search the Internet or magazines for pictures. Print or cut them out to fill the pages. Or draw your own!

Boiled peanuts are South Carolina's official snack.

Pet and feed goats at the South Carolina State Fair petting zoo.

25

SOUTH CAROLINA BY MAP

> MAP KEY

- ⬟ Capital city
- ◯ City
- ◉ Point of interest
- ▲ Highest elevation
- – · – State border
- ▬▬ Cherokee Foothills National Scenic Highway

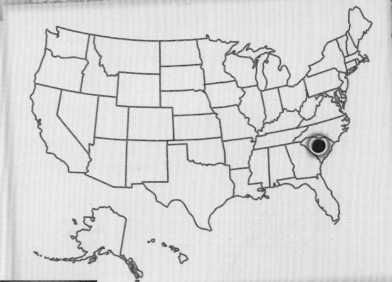

Visit www.lerneresource.com to learn more about the state flag of South Carolina.

APPALACHIAN MOUNTAINS

Table Rock State Park

Sassafras Mountain
(3,560 feet/
1,085 m)

Hollywild
Animal Park
(Wellford)

Greenville

Rock
Hill

Oconee State Park

NORTH CAROLINA

Great Pee Dee River

PIEDMONT PLATEAU

N

Savannah River

Columbia

Sumter

Grand Strand

Hawaiian Rumble
Mini Golf

Congaree
National
Park

(North Fork)

(South Fork)

Santee River

Myrtle Beach

GEORGIA

ATLANTIC
OCEAN

Edisto River

Goose Creek

Summerville

Mount
Pleasant

North Charleston

Charleston

Boone Hall
Plantation
& Gardens

Gullah Festival
(Beaufort)

Fort Sumter
(Charleston Harbor)

Sea Pines
Forest Preserve

South Carolina Aquarium

Middleton Place

Magnolia Plantation
& Gardens

Hilton Head
Island

Miles
0   20   40   60

0   40   80
Kilometers

SOUTH CAROLINA FACTS

NICKNAMES: Palmetto State, the Rice State

SONG: "Carolina" by Henry Timrod and Anne Custis Burgess

MOTTOS: *Animis opibusque parati*, or "Prepared in mind and resources"; *Dum spiro spero*, or "While I breathe, I hope"

> **FLOWER:** Carolina yellow jessamine

TREE: palmetto

> **BIRD:** Carolina wren

ANIMAL: white-tailed deer

FOOD: boiled peanuts

DATE AND RANK OF STATEHOOD: May 23, 1788; the 8th state

> **CAPITAL:** Columbia

AREA: 31,114 square miles (80,585 sq. km)

AVERAGE JANUARY TEMPERATURE: 45°F (7°C)

AVERAGE JULY TEMPERATURE: 80°F (27°C)

POPULATION AND RANK: 4,774,839; 24th (2013)

MAJOR CITIES AND POPULATIONS: Columbia (131,686), Charleston (125,583), North Charleston (101,989), Mount Pleasant (71,875), Rock Hill (68,094)

NUMBER OF US CONGRESS MEMBERS: 7 representatives, 2 senators

NUMBER OF ELECTORAL VOTES: 9

NATURAL RESOURCES: rich soils, kaolin clay, limestone, gold, granite, talc, pine, oak, bay trees, palmettos

> **AGRICULTURAL PRODUCTS:** cotton, rice, corn, chickens, turkeys, hogs

MANUFACTURED GOODS: chemicals, textiles, wood, pulp, paper products

STATE HOLIDAYS AND CELEBRATIONS: South Carolina State Fair, Confederate Memorial Day, Gullah Festival, Penn Center Heritage Days Celebration

GLOSSARY

culture: the ideas, beliefs, and way of life of a group of people

descendant: a family member who lived in the past

economy: the system of making, selling, and buying products and resources

erupt: to suddenly explode upward with steam, lava, or fire

heritage: traditions and beliefs that groups of people believe are important to their history

palmetto: a type of palm tree

plantation: a large crop farm located in a warm climate

plateau: a large area of flat ground that is higher than the ground surrounding it

secede: to exit from a group or organization, often with the purpose of forming a different group or organization

traditional: having to do with a custom or belief that is handed down through generations

LERNER

SOURCE™

Expand learning beyond the printed book. Download free, complementary educational resources for this book from our website, www.lerneresource.com.

FURTHER INFORMATION

Gullah Net
http://www.knowitall.org/gullahnet
Read or listen to Aunt Pearlie Sue tell Gullah stories. Learn how to pronounce
Gullah words and hear Gullah music. You can also look up Gullah events
happening in South Carolina.

Jerome, Kate Boehm. *Charleston, SC: Cool Stuff Every Kid Should Know*.
Charleston SC: Arcadia, 2008. Find tons of facts about the city of Charleston.
This book includes info on history, funny facts, and city landmarks.

Kent, Zachary. *The Civil War: From Fort Sumter to Appomattox*. Berkeley
Heights, NJ: Enslow, 2011. Learn more about the battle fought at Fort Sumter
and the US Civil War that followed.

Knudsen, Shannon. *When Were the First Slaves Set Free during the Civil War?*
Minneapolis: Lerner Publications, 2011. Learn more about why slavery was
so important to the southern states and how the slaves were finally freed.

National Park Service, South Carolina
http://www.nps.gov/state/sc/index.htm?program=all
South Carolina has many state parks. Find them on a map, read about their
features, and plan your visit!

Netstate: South Carolina
http://www.netstate.com/states/intro/sc_intro.htm
Find tons of facts about South Carolina's geography, people, population,
weather, state symbols, and more. Take a state quiz to test how much
you know!

INDEX

PHOTO ACKNOWLEDGMENTS

The images in this book are used with the permission of: © StacieStauffSmith Photos /Shutterstock Images, pp. 1, 6–7; NASA, pp. 2–3; © Konstantin L/Shutterstock Images, p. 4; © Dave Allen Photography/Shutterstock Images, pp. 5 (bottom), 8–9; © Laura Westlund/Independent Picture Service, pp. 5 (top), 27; © Phil McDonald/Shutterstock Images, p. 7 (right); Clair P, p. 7 (left); © Fotoluminate LLC/Shutterstock Images, p. 9 (top); © Pat Canova/Alamy, p. 9 (bottom); © Gabrielle Hovey/Shutterstock Images, pp. 10–11, 29 (bottom right); Carol M Highsmith Archive/Library of Congress, p. 11 (left) (LC-DIG-highsm-12487); National Park Service, p. 11 (right); © Brad Sauter/Shutterstock Images, pp. 12–13; © Louise Heusinkveld /Alamy, p. 13 (right); © Raffaella Calzoni /Shutterstock Images, p. 13 (left); © Bob Krist /Corbis, p. 14; © Richard Ellis/Alamy, pp. 14–15; © bddigitalimages/Shutterstock Images, p. 15; © Serge the Photographer /Shutterstock Images, pp. 16–17; © Shutterstock Images, pp. 17 (left), 17 (right), 24–25, 29 (top right); © Patryk Kosmider /Shutterstock Images, pp. 18–19; © Volodymyr Burdiak/Shutterstock Images, p. 18; © Nate Allred/Shutterstock Images, p. 19; © Ken Thomas, pp. 20–21; © Jason Tench /Shutterstock Images, p. 21 (bottom); US Fish and Wildlife Service, p. 21 (top); © Jorg Hackemann/Shutterstock Images, pp. 22–23; © Pat & Chuck Blackley/Alamy, p. 23 (top); Library of Congress, p. 23 (bottom) (LC-USZC4-7969); © Joe Mercier/Shutterstock Images, p. 25 (right); © Thanatip S. /Shutterstock Images, p. 25 (left); © nicoolay /iStockphoto, p. 26; © Steve Byland /Shutterstock Images, p. 29 (top left); © Paul Matthew Photography/Shutterstock Images, p. 29 (bottom left).

Cover: © Beth Whitcomb/Shutterstock.com (cannon); © Alexander Glagolev/Dreamstime .com (sailboat); iStockphoto.com /DenisTangneyJr, (Myrtle Beach); © Daveallenphoto/Dreamstime.com (Table Rock State Park); © Laura Westlund /Independent Picture Service (map); © iStockphoto.com/fpm (seal); © iStockphoto .com/vicm (pushpins); © iStockphoto.com /benz190 (corkboard).